The Mary Rose Story

The Mary Rose Story

John Christopher

Northumberland County Council	
3 0132 02113231 6	
Askews & Holts	Jun-2012
623.822	£8.99

The History Press

Published in the United Kingdom in 2012 by
The History Press
The Mill · Brimscombe Port · Stroud · Gloucestershire · GL5 2QG

British Library Cataloguing in Publication Data
A catalogue record for this book is available from the British
Library.

Hardback ISBN 978-0-7524-6404-6

Half Title page: *Still sailing, a* Mary Rose
weathervane. (Basphoto)

Half Title verso: *Several musical instruments were
recovered from the wreck including a shawm, an
oboe-like instrument shown here with a replica, and
a pair of tabor pipes.*

Typesetting and origination by The History Press
Manufacturing managed by Jellyfish Print Solutions Ltd
Printed in India

CONTENTS

ACKNOWLEDGEMENTS

I am very grateful to the following for additional photographs: The Mary Rose Trust, the US Library of Congress, Andreas Praefcke, Campbell McCutcheon (J.&C. McCutcheon Collection), Peter Isolto and Basphoto. Other new photography is by the author. I must also thank the staff at Portsmouth's Historic Dockyard for their kind assistance, and thanks also to my wife, Ute, for her continued support and many hours of proof reading.

A number of sources have been consulted in the production of this book, including: *The Mary Rose – The Excavation and Raising of Henry VIII's Flagship* by Margaret Rule, *Great Harry's Navy* by Geoffrey Moorhouse, *The Book of British Ships* by Frank H. Mason, *Sealed by Time – The Loss and Recovery of the Mary Rose* by Peter Marsden, and *Shipping Wonders of the World* edited by Clarence Winchester.

➤ *An oar-powered galley or row-barge.*

Your good ship, the flower, I trow, of all ships that ever sailed.

Sir Edward Howard writing to Henry VIII in praise of the *Mary Rose*

Not since the wedding of Prince Charles to Lady Diana Spencer in 1981, or the Apollo 11 Moon landing of 1969, had so many people, up to 60 million some say, stopped what they were doing to gather around their television sets. But this time there was no fairy-tale State ceremony filling the screen, nor the historic image of a ghostly figure, blurred by vast distance, stepping on to the lunar soil. Instead they watched in anticipation as events unfolded on the Solent, the narrow strip of water that separates the Isle of Wight from the English mainland. It was early on the morning of Monday 11 October 1982 and another epic journey was reaching its conclusion. Not a journey to another world separated by space, but to one separated by time.

It had been 437 years earlier on a balmy summer's day in July 1545 that King Henry VIII's fleet, including the flagship *Mary Rose*, had prepared to repel a French invasion force that had gathered at the eastern mouth to the Solent. Conditions had been very calm at first and as the French oar-powered galleys harried the defenders, the English captains struggled to make any progress in the confined waters. Towards the evening the wind picked up a little and the *Mary Rose* took the lead. What happened next is uncertain. It is thought she fired a starboard broadside at the French vessels and had started to come about, either to present the guns on the other side or to avoid the sandbanks, when the breeze caught her sails causing the ship to heel over. The water poured in through the open lower gunports and suddenly and unexpectedly the *Mary Rose* sank with the loss of all but thirty-five of a crew estimated at over 400 men. Watching from Southsea Castle, King Henry had seen the ship sink and he heard the desperate cries of the crew trapped beneath nets which were supposed to keep boarders off the open decks. In disbelief he was heard to say, 'Oh, my gallant men! Oh, my gallant men.'

Four centuries later, it was a very different audience that watched as the wreck of the *Mary Rose* was raised from the murky waters. At first only the top of the yellow lifting frame broke the surface and then, little by little, the remains of the ship came into view. Suddenly there was a crunching sound. A retaining pin had snapped and one corner of the supporting framework lurched downwards, threatening to crush its precious cargo. The faces of the recovery team were momentarily frozen in shock, but no damage had been done and by the end of the day the *Mary Rose* had been safely towed into Portsmouth harbour.

Raising the *Mary Rose* had been an incredible endeavour, a huge team effort and a milestone in the field of maritime archaeology. Perhaps many of the television viewers who arrived late to work or school that morning had been a little bit disappointed as they had expected to see something that looked more like a

Tudor warship emerging from the waters, but it is only when the remains of the ship and the thousands of recovered artefacts are seen alongside each other that we can truly appreciate its significance. The *Mary Rose* is, to coin a much over-used phrase, a wonderful time capsule – a unique slice of life in the sixteenth century.

John Christopher, 2011

One of the Mary Rose's *cast bronze guns on a replica carriage.*

Henry VIII was not slow to realize that riches could be obtained only by seafaring, yet English seamanhood at that time was numerically small and generally ignorant … Henry therefore introduced a scheme of nautical education …

Shipping Wonders of the World

Just eighteen years old when he ascended to the throne in 1509, King Henry VIII – popularly known as Harry – was a handsome, charismatic young man. The clichéd image we have of the bloated, hedonistic glutton only applies to his later life. Instead, in his prime we have a young king who was athletic and excelled at hunting and jousting. Well-educated, he was widely acclaimed as an accomplished musician and composer, author and poet. He also took a particular interest in his navy. Not the normal level of interest any responsible king might take, but a close and personal interest in every aspect of the ships and their weaponry.

In 1509 Henry had inherited a force of around fifteen ships from his father, Henry VII, including the *Regent* of 1,000 tons and the *Sovereign* of 800 tons. Typically such large ships would serve a dual purpose as merchantmen in time of peace and were fitted with relatively small guns arranged on the upper decks in times of war. While this arrangement gave some advantage in terms of height from which to fire upon the enemy, it did limit the weight of the guns which could be carried. It was only with the development of the gunport that larger guns could be carried on lower decks. The inherited fleet had several smaller ships too,

such as the *Mary and John*, *Sweepstake* and *Mary Fortune*. Henry also benefited from his father's prudent measures to protect the nation's maritime interests with, for example, improvements made to the defences at Portsmouth harbour, the main naval base on the south coast, and in 1495 the excavation of the first dry dock, located on Portsea Island. Prior to that it had been traditional practice to build ships on the shoreline where the work was at the mercy of the tides. The dry dock also provided the only way to overhaul the hulls of larger vessels such as the *Regent* and *Sovereign*, which were too big to be hauled up on to the shore. All in all, his father had provided the young Henry with a solid enough foundation on which to build a new navy, although admittedly a sustained period of political calm on the high seas was reflected

◄ *King Henry VIII has been credited with laying the foundations of what became the Royal Navy.*

in the relatively small scale of the fleet. With the new king on the throne that was all about to change; the sixteenth century would experience much stormier waters.

At the start of Henry's reign in 1509, England had lost most of its vast continental possessions and retained only a precarious toe-hold on Calais. England was only a minor power compared with Europe's prime movers Spain, the Holy Roman Empire and France. These three had become involved in the War of the League of Cambrai in 1508, a conflict initially aimed at the Republic of Venice but later turned against the French. England had close ties with the Spanish and six weeks into his reign Henry married the Spanish princess Catherine of Aragon in order to strengthen his alliance in a bid to reaffirm and support his claim as king of both England and France. And indeed, by

1511 England was part of the anti-French alliance. It was against this background that Henry implemented a ship-building programme to greatly strengthen the navy and to protect the country from its near neighbours, not only the French but also the Scots whose ships had been harrying English vessels in what was little more than open piracy.

Fortunately for Henry his father had left him with a considerable personal fortune with which he could indulge his interests, in particular building palaces – over forty new ones during his reign – and ships. Within months of his accession, Henry VIII authorised the construction of two large warships at Portsmouth. Evidence suggests that these were the *Mary Rose* of 500 tons and the *Peter Pomegranate* – most likely named after Saint Peter and the pomegranate badge of Queen Catherine of Aragon and later known simply as the *Peter* – of 450 tons. It is possible that they were based on plans already instigated by his father, but it was certainly Henry VIII who oversaw the project. Many more ships followed, most notably the massive *Henry Grace à Dieu*, or 'Henry Grace of God' which was commonly referred to simply as the 'Great Harry', of 1,000-ton burden, built at the Woolwich dockyard and launched in 1514. Not content in simply ordering new ships, the king also turned his hand to designing ships himself and it is thought that he was the architect of the oar-powered *Rose in the Sun* which, at 20 tons burden and with a crew of around forty men, was one of the smallest vessels in the English fleet. Much favoured by the Mediterranean countries, the advantage

◄ *Hans Holbein the Younger's depiction of a carrack-style merchant ship. Until the establishment of a permanent navy it was common practice to arm merchant vessels when needed.*

of galleys or row-barges is that they could operate in shallower coastal waters and in the sort of calmer conditions that rendered the bigger sail-powered vessels immobile.

The expansion of English sea-power continued throughout Henry's reign and when an illustrated inventory of his ships, known as the Anthony Roll, was presented to the king in 1546 it depicted fifty-eight vessels. The list featured all sizes and types of ships from the massive *Henry Grace*

◀ *A dramatic representation of the* Great Harry, *the largest ship in Henry VIII's fleet.*

▶ *The flagship* Henry Grace á Dieu, *or 'Henry Grace of God', was also known as the 'Great Harry' after the king.*

An illustration of the Swallow *from the* Anthony Roll *which was a visual inventory of Henry VIII's ships.*

It is believed that Henry VIII may have designed the Rose in the Sun, *an oar-powered galley or row-barge, shown here on the* Anthony Roll.

à Dieu to the oar-powered *Rose in the Sun*. The inclusion of the *Mary Rose* is of particular interest, especially as the Roll was completed a year after she had sunk. It is quite possible that the *Mary Rose* was included because that part of the roll had been completed before the sinking, or because the roll represented an overall view of built ships, active or not. Another intriguing theory is that the *Mary Rose*'s appearance on the roll indicates that they still expected her to be salvaged.

Beyond the ship-building programme, Henry VIII also recognised the need to better organise, equip and train his navy, as well as providing an improved support infrastructure. He invested heavily in the dockyards and strengthened the coastal defences, and it was under Henry that the English foundries developed blast furnaces

for casting iron guns which were far cheaper than the prevailing bronze cannon (*see* Chapter 3, A Ship of War). Henry also encouraged the formation of a seaman's guild, known as Trinity House, to foster navigational skills and provide almshouses for the needy. Most significantly, his reign marked the move away from a ramshackle naval force drawn together at times of need from poorly equipped merchant vessels, to a dedicated 'Navy Royal' with its own core of warships. It might still have lacked the formal structure that we would recognise today, but King Henry's navy marked the rise of English sea-power. It was a key factor in repelling the Spanish Armada later in the sixteenth century, and it sowed the seeds of what later became the Royal Navy.

◄ *A scale model of the* Mary Rose *as she would have appeared at the time of the Battle of the Solent.*

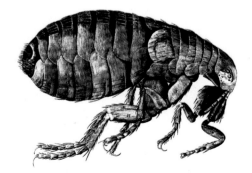

19

> Was told by a Fleming among the survivors that when she heeled over with the wind, the water entered by the lowest row of gunports which had been left open after firing.

Van der Delft, Imperial Ambassador, on the sinking of the *Mary Rose*

The *Mary Rose* was one of Henry VIII's new breed of purpose-built warships. Prior to this it had been customary to hire merchant ships in time of war and to hire out naval ships in the intervening peace. Construction of the *Mary Rose* commenced in 1510 at the Portsmouth dockyard and she was launched in July the following year. The ship was then towed to London where she was fitted out with decking, armaments, rigging and other equipment. There has been some debate about the origin of the ship's name. It has frequently been stated that the ship was named after the king's favourite sister, Mary Tudor, together with the Tudor rose emblem.

However, some historians have questioned this explanation saying that there is no hard evidence to support it and they think it more likely that the ship was named after the Virgin Mary.

The *Mary Rose* is a carrack-style ship, from the Spanish word *carraca* or the French equivalent *caraque*, a design which originated in the Mediterranean and was typified by the ships which Columbus sailed across the Atlantic in 1492. (A hundred years later, by the end of the sixteenth century, the carrack had evolved into the galleon with a longer hull and lower superstructure.) The carrack has an elegant profile, as seen on the surviving section

➤ *The most famous image of the* Mary Rose *comes from the Anthony Roll. It shows the ship after her 1536 refit, although some of the detailing is questionable.*

◄ *A late fifteenth-century Flemish carrack, a style of ship which influenced the design of the* Mary Rose. *Note the rounded stern.*

► *The traditional method of ship construction was on the river bank, but this left the workings exposed to the tides. To overcome this Henry VIII had the first dry dock built at Portsmouth.*

of the *Mary Rose*, which curves upwards at the bow and stern. In cross-section the hull shape is known as a 'tumblehorn' form, with the widest part at the waterline and tapering inwards towards the top to compensate for the weight of the guns

▶ *Sir Walter Raleigh's* Ark Royal *was built more than forty years after the loss of the* Mary Rose, *but this illustration shows the influence of the four-masted carrack design with high stern castle.*

▶▶ *Christopher Columbus's famous* Santa Maria *was a small carrack, about 70ft long, built around 1480. This is a twentieth-century replica of the famous ship. (Library of Congress)*

and to make it more difficult for enemy soldiers to board the ship. The castles at the bow and stern rise up high to provide a vantage point for the archers firing down upon an enemy's vessels. The low gap in the middle of the ship, between the fore and stern castles and known as the 'waist', was covered over with netting as a defence against boarders.

The *Mary Rose* was not the biggest warship in Henry's fleet, as that honour went to the *Henry Grace à Dieu*, but she was certainly one of the bigger ones. There are no precise measurements, but examination of the remains suggests that she was 126ft (38.5m) long at the waterline and her draught (the depth of water required to float the hull) was 15ft (4.6m). It is estimated that 600 trees, mostly mature oaks and covering some forty acres,

were needed for her construction. By the sixteenth century the larger oaks trees were becoming increasingly rare locally and the timber was brought to Portsmouth from forests all over southern England. The keel is made from three pieces of elm scarfed together, a method of joining members end to end, to give a length of 104ft (32m). It is thought that the *Mary Rose* underwent two major refits or rebuilds during her career, one at Portsmouth in 1527–28 and the other in the Thames in or around 1536. The ship's burden was increased from 500 to 700 tons, most probably in the later refit, and there is evidence that substantial

◀ *Was the* Mary Rose *named after the king's sister Princess Mary? This portrait shows Mary with her second husband Charles Brandon, Duke of Suffolk, after their marriage in 1515.*

▲ *The way of constructing the wooden ships has hardly changed and these illustrations from the late eighteenth century show carpenters working with hand tools.*

27

➤ Looking towards
the stern, the recovered
starboard section
of the Mary Rose at
Portsmouth's dockyard.
The yellow steelwork
is the support cradle in
which she was raised
from the seabed.
(The Mary Rose Trust)

strengthening was added to the hull. Again this was probably during the 1536 refit to allow for the greater weight which had to be carried. One major innovation in the construction of the ship was the change from a traditional clinker-built hull, where the planks overlap, to carvel construction methods with the planks butting edge-to-edge. The result was a smooth-sided hull, allowing the installation of gunports on several decks for the first time (*see* Chapter 3, A Ship of War).

The hull had four levels: At the top was the open weatherdeck, or upper deck, exposed to the elements. Leading off from the upper deck and beneath the stern castle structure there was accommodation for the crew. Working downwards, the main deck is next. This was a continuous deck that housed the heaviest guns – seven gunports to either side – plus cabins located at the rear beneath the stern castle. Next comes the orlop, or 'overlop', a storage area for spare sails, food and equipment, and finally the hold at the bottom of the ship below the waterline. The hold would have contained ballast and the heavy stores, plus the ship's magazine – the store for gunpowder. The kitchen or galley was also located within the hold, but well away from the magazine.

The *Mary Rose* had four masts, plus a bowsprit pointing forwards from the bow, and nine or possibly ten sails would have been flown from these. The masts were named from the bow working backwards as the foremast, the mainmast which was the tallest, the mizzenmast and lastly the bonaventure mizzen mast at the back. Extending horizontally from the stern was a

short boon known as an outligger. Each of the vertical masts had one or sometimes two mast tops, and the crow's nest of popular fiction, to be used by a lookout. Holding the masts in place was the standing rigging, a permanent network of ropes or lines attached to a wide wooden strip or plank known as a chain-wale, later shortened to 'channel', which ran horizontally along the side of the upper hull or stern castle.

When it came to performance the *Mary Rose* was considered to be one of the finest ships in the fleet. Sir Edward Howard once described her to the king as, 'Your good ship, the flower, I trow, of all ships that ever sailed"

◄ *Another ocean-going carrack, this time Portuguese explorer Vasco de Gama's* São Gabriel *in which he sailed around Africa to India in 1497–99. (Library of Congress)*

◄ *A selection of the ship's wooden blocks and pulley gear on display at the Mary Rose Museum. These continued to be made by hand until Marc Brunel installed his block-making machinery at Portsmouth in the nineteenth century.*

… firing any heavy guns from somewhere below the weather deck through ports cut into each side of a ship was considered a very serious (even daring) departure from traditional design and practice in 1511.

Geoffrey Moorhouse, *Great Harry's Navy*

The early sixteenth century was a transitional period in the design of fighting ships which saw their evolution from floating platforms from which the soldiers fought at close hand with conventional weapons, to purpose-built warships that bristled with guns. The driving force behind this change was the rapid advances in the casting and manufacture of the guns. As they got bigger and heavier they needed to be placed lower within the hull and, consequently, closer to the waterline.

The *Mary Rose* was equipped with two main types of guns, iron breech-loaders and cast bronze muzzle-loaders. The breech-loader was the earlier type and was made up of iron bars which had been formed into cylinders, welded together and reinforced with iron hoops to make the long barrel. They were fitted with several chambers which held the gun powder charge. Being breech-loaded meant that there was no need to withdraw the gun from the gunport after each firing. This made the iron guns much quicker to reload, but as they took less powerful charges than the bronze guns their range was shorter. In general they fired stone shot which was designed to shatter on impact with devastating results on personnel and rigging.

➤ *Gun furniture: A ladle for gunpowder, at the top, the nozzle from a powder flask; the long stick is a linstock which held a length of slow-burning rope to fire the gun, plus a primer needle to clear the touch hole, tampions inserted after the powder and shot, and the round shot itself. (The Mary Rose Trust)*

33

➤ *A stack of stone shot which was designed to shatter, causing maximum damage.*

➤➤ *Decorative detail on cast bronze guns from the* Mary Rose. *Henry VIII encouraged the European gun foundries to come to England to ensure a secure supply of the large guns.*

Bronze guns, on the other hand, were cast in a single piece which made them far stronger. The bronze guns were used at greater range and generally fired iron shot to penetrate an enemy's hull. The introduction of gunports made coordinated

IRON DICE-SHOT – for use with the
hailshot piece

HAILSHOT PIECE – cast iron, muzzle
loading. These were recovered, all from
the starboard.

volleys known as broadsides possible for the first time. Prior to that the heaviest guns had been carried in the bows of galleys, facing forward and aimed by turning the vessel to either side. In contrast, the broadside delivered a far wider spread of shot in one go. The disadvantage of the muzzle-loaded bronze guns meant that they had to be withdrawn from the gunports to allow access for reloading. In theory while this was being done the ship could be turned 180 degrees to fire a broadside from the loaded guns on the other side, and it has been suggested that the *Mary Rose* may have been carrying out this manoeuvre when she heeled over and water entered through the lower gunports.

During the excavation of the wreck both types of guns were found on the starboard

◀◀ *On display at Portsmouth, examples of an iron breech-loaded swivel gun, and on the right the smaller muzzle-loaded hailshot piece.*

◀ *This beautifully ornate lion's head is a lifting ring on one of the cast bronze guns.*

side of the main deck, and others were located on the upper and rear castle decks. At least one of the guns on the castle deck faced forward, possibly to deal with forward-firing galleys. The illustration of the *Mary Rose* on the Anthony Roll depicts three rows of guns on the side of the hull with more guns on the forecastle and eight firing backwards from the stern. The ship was also equipped with two types of lighter guns. Breech-loaded iron guns which were located in the castles and upper decks and were swivel mounted so they could be aimed by the gunner. The other was a blunt cast-iron gun, muzzle-loaded, which fired hailshot at a close range as an anti-personnel weapon.

The exact type and distribution of the guns on the *Mary Rose* would have altered throughout her lifetime and it seems certain that the number of guns was increased during the 1536 refit. Examples of all of the types of gun mentioned were retrieved from the wreck including ten magnificent cast bronze guns. These are beautiful objects, personalised in their castings with the Tudor rose emblem, or lions' heads

Did you know?

The Portuguese explorer Ferdinand Magellan completed the first circumnavigation of the world in 1522, just ten years after the *Mary Rose* was fitted out.

HENRYCVS·OCLAVꝰ·DE·Iꝰ
GRACIA·ANGLIE·ET·FRAN
CIE·REX·FIDEI·DEFENSOR
DNS·HIBERNIE·ET·IN·TER
RA·SVPREꝰ·V·CAP·EC
CLESIE·ANGLICANE

➤ Hand weapons were vital in repelling the enemy at close quarters. This soldier is armed with a traditional long pike.

for lifting lugs, or inscriptions. The king had encouraged continental gun founders to settle in England and one large gun, known as a 'Bastard Culverin' – bastard indicating that it is non-standard and culverin denoting its size – was cast by the Houndsditch Foundry in London. It is displayed on a replica four-wheel gun carriage, and on the casting itself there is an inscription or dedication that sums up the king's political ambitions at the time. Translated from the Latin it reads:

> HENRY THE EIGHTH BY THE GRACE OF GOD, KING OF ENGLAND AND FRANCE, DEFENDER OF THE FAITH, LORD OF IRELAND AND ON EARTH SUPREME HEAD OF THE CHURCH OF ENGLAND.

HAND-TO-HAND WARFARE

The longbow had been one of the most important weapons of medieval times, both on land and at sea, and the English continued to use them well into the sixteenth century. Archery was mandatory for able-bodied men in Tudor times and it is thought that around 250 longbows were carried on the *Mary Rose*. Of these, 137 examples have been recovered intact along with more than 3,500 arrows, most of which were stored in wooden chests either in the orlop or on the upper deck. The bow staves were made from a single baulk of yew, retaining the natural laminate of heartwood and sapwood for greater strength. They were shaped to a D-section with a flat back of sapwood and the rounded centre of heartwood. Average length of the long bows was 6.5ft (1.98m). The arrows were mostly of poplar, with some examples in beech, ash and hazel. Other recovered archery equipment included leather wrist-guards and circular arrow spacers to hold twenty-four arrows in readiness. Because of their length the longbows could only have been drawn on the top decks, the archers protected by a series of moveable wooden panels or blinds fitted along the side railings and made of poplar which is less likely to splinter than oak.

Hand-held guns in the form of matchlock muskets would have been on board the Tudor warships and during the remainder of the sixteenth century they came to replace the longbows. The Anthony Roll suggests that fifty of these guns were carried and archaeologists have found the complete stocks of five muskets and fragments from another eleven. Intriguingly

they also discovered several rare examples of gunshields, wooden disks with a hole in the middle through which to fire.

As a defence against boarding, the ship carried a large number of mêlée or close contact weapons including very long

thrusting spears known as pikes, and bills which had shorter staffs with a metal axe blade or hook at the end. So many examples of pikes were found on the upper deck of the wreck, ready for action, that the area became known as the 'pike garden' among the archaeologists. Bladed weapons such as swords and daggers were also on the wreck and these would have been the personal possessions of the crew. The wooden handles from sixty-six 'ballock' or kidney daggers were recovered, plus a number of sword handles, although only one sword is complete with its blade.

◄ *The soldiers would have been involved in bitter close combat, as depicted in this contemporary engraving by Hans Burgmair the Elder of a battle on the Danube, c.1514.*

Guns were placed not merely in the bows … but also along either side of the hull as well as at the stern. The greatest concentration of fire, therefore, came not when the ship was bows-on towards the enemy, but with her broadside exposed.

Shipping Wonders of the World

In the autumn of 1511, when the new warship *Mary Rose* was still being fitted out, the political situation in Europe took a new turn that drew England into a series of conflicts with France. The Pope and the King of Aragon had formed an alliance against Louis XXII of France and in January 1512 the English Parliament agreed to join with the Spanish against the French. It was decided that while the Spanish attacked them in the Bay of Biscay and Gascony, the English would hold the Channel and keep it clear of enemy ships in preparation for an assault on Boulogne. In April 1512, Henry appointed Sir Edward Howard as Lord High Admiral. Howard chose the newly completed *Mary Rose* as his flagship with a fleet of eighteen vessels including the *Regent* and *Peter Pomegranate*.

Over the next two months Howard's forces cleared the Channel and captured twelve Breton ships. In June they returned to Portsmouth to take part in a Royal Fleet Review attended by the king. Then in August the English ships set sail again, this time for Brest where they encountered a joint French-Breton fleet of over 200 ships anchored close to the shore. Prominent among them was the *Grande Louise*, the flagship of the French Admiral René

Did you know?
At the time when the *Mary Rose* was built the population of England was around 3 million. That's less than half of the number of people living in today's Greater London.

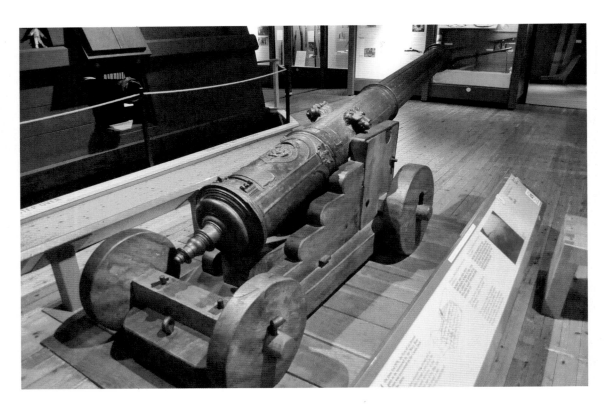

◄◄ A large bronze cannon displayed on a replica gun carriage. Because they were muzzle-loaded these guns had to be withdrawn from the gunports for reloading.

◄ The only example of a sixteenth-century mast top. It survived because it was stored as a spare in the forward part of the hull.

de Clermont. Howard in the *Mary Rose* engaged the Breton flagship *Cordelière*, immediately bombarded the *Grande* ably assisted by archers on the *Regent* *Louise*, while the smaller *Mary James* which had come alongside it. The Breton ship caught fire, whether set alight by English fire arrows or by its own crew unwilling to surrender is uncertain. The *Cordelière*'s magazine went up in a violent explosion and both the *Cordelière* and the *Regent* were destroyed in the conflagration with the loss of hundreds of men including the High Admiral of France. In further encounters the English burnt twenty-seven French vessels and captured five, and a raiding party landed near Brest before bad weather forced the fleet back to England.

In the spring of 1513 the *Mary Rose* was back in action against the French at Brest, only this time the French fleet had been strengthened by the arrival of galleys brought up from the Mediterranean. The galleys sank one English ship and damaged another. After launching a fruitless land assault against Brest, Howard resorted to a daring frontal attack with a force of small oared vessels. It went horribly wrong and, separated from the other English ships, Howard was killed. Having lost its admiral, the fleet returned to England. Minor skirmishes continued throughout the following summer of 1514, but by the autumn the war was over with the peace sealed by the marriage of Henry's sister Mary to Louis XII.

In 1522 conflict with France flared up again, this time because of a treaty with the Holy Roman Emperor Charles V, and the *Mary Rose* participated in the escort transport of troops in the summer of 1522. From then until 1545 the *Mary Rose* was placed 'in ordinary', in other words in reserves. During that time little is known about her activities except that she underwent repairs and in 1536 she

was refitted and partially rebuilt with modifications made to her gun decks to house bigger cannon. Some experts suggest that it was only then that the hull construction was changed from clinker built to carvel planking, and before that date the ship may have more closely resembled a fifteenth-century-style warship with rounded stern and no main deck gunports.

◄ *Soldiers armed with a selection of deadly weapons. From the left, the bill with its metal axe head or hook, then the long pike and half pike.*

► *The introduction of gunports enabled the ships to fire broadsides, but the action was still at close range as shown in this painting from the early seventeenth century.*

51

Henry VIII's Dissolution of the Monasteries in 1534 and his subsequent excommunication from the Church in Rome, combined with the annulment of his marriage to Catherine of Aragon, aunt to the Holy Roman Emperor Charles V, left the Tudor king increasingly isolated. Political alliances within Europe were in a state of flux and the threat of a combined attack by French and Spanish forces prompted Henry to launch an intensive programme of improvements to the coastal fortifications

◄ A royal coat of arms on one of the cast bronze guns.

on the southern coast, including Southsea Castle which was completed in 1544. With his 'homeland security' in place Henry launched an attack against France and captured Boulogne, at enormous cost, but he was left in the lurch when the other protagonists brokered their own peace agreement. Then in May 1545 the French assembled a vast invasion fleet of up to 300 vessels in the Seine estuary, plus a force of between 30,000 to 50,000 troops at Le Havre, with a view to landing on English soil.

By early June 1545 the English fleet, under Viscount Lisle, had mustered 160 ships and 12,000 troops at Portsmouth. Before the French were ready to sail Henry launched a pre-emptive strike which proved to be ineffective, and in early July the French, under the command of admiral Claude D'Annebault, set sail for England. On 18 July 1545 they entered the Solent where they expected to encounter the English warships, including the *Mary Rose*, at anchorage in Portsmouth harbour.

If any man kill another within the ship, he that doeth the deed shall be bound quick to the dead man, and so be cast into the sea, and a piece of ordnance be shot off after they be thrown into the sea. If any man draw a weapon within the ship to strike his captain, he shall lose his right hand.

Orders to be used in the King Majesty's Navy by the Sea

Estimates of the number of crew on board a ship such as the *Mary Rose* vary. The Anthony Roll states that the crew consisted of 200 mariners, 185 soldiers and 30 gunners, giving a total of just over 400 which is consistent with other records. When taking part in land invasions or raids this number was likely to have been swelled by additional soldiers and the combined total could have reached 700 men.

For much of her career the *Mary Rose* acted as a flagship with the Lord High Admiral or vice-admiral on board, and Vice-Admiral George Carew is the only positively identified person to have gone down with the ship in July 1545. In charge of the ship was the captain, a highly prestigious position on such an important ship and they were usually appointed from the gentry or aristocracy, people such as Sir William Fitzwilliam and Sir Thomas Wyndham. Under the captain was the master, a professional seaman who was in charge of the sailing of the ship, and he was assisted by the boatswain, master's mates and quartermasters. Other officers included the purser, master gunner, carpenter, surgeon, steward and cook. The ordinary mariners were a class apart, probably made up of professional seamen

together with men escaping the poverty of working on the land. On board ship they had regular food and drink, and analysis of the skeletons discovered during excavations reveals that most were well-fed young men under thirty years of age. A disproportionate number suffered from a condition known as os acromiale which affects the shoulder blades and is common among archers.

◀ *A wooden lantern.*

▲ *The ordinary crew members would have drunk from simple wooden tankards and eaten from wooden plates.*

One of the three compasses carried on the Mary Rose.

NAVIGATION

The sixteenth-century mariners lacked many of the important navigational tools of later centuries, such as telescopes, barometers and chronometers. However, they did have the basics including compasses, sounding leads to determine the depth in shallower waters, and instruments in the form of early sextants known as a cross staff which were used for measuring the angle of the sun, moon and stars, although none of these instruments was found on the wreck. They also had rudimentary charts and associated equipment such as dividers and a plotting board. To measure their speed through the water a log was attached to the end of a long line calibrated with knots and paid out from a wooden reel. The number of knots reeled in a given time, measured by an hour glass, gave the speed in knots, a term still in use today.

HEALTH

The barber-surgeon played a vital role on any warship, tending to the wounded in time of battle and dealing with sick crewmen to prevent the rapid spread of infection or disease in the cramped and overcrowded conditions. He would have been a highly skilled professional and in 1540 the king had presented a charter to the Guild of Barber Surgeons. The remains of the barber-surgeon's cabin were found on the starboard side of the main deck, close to the action, and working with assistants he would have performed amputations, set broken bones and cauterised wounds to aid healing. Among the finds from the wreck was the barber-surgeon's wooden chest holding his medicines and equipment including the handles from a complete set of surgical tools, a copper syringe, shaving bowls, combs and ear-scoops, plus five German-made corked jars for medicines and ointments.

FOOD AND DRINK

Because the *Mary Rose* was a warship and hence not required to undertake long voyages to distant parts of the globe, she would have been resupplied on a regular basis. This meant that the crew did not suffer the conditions normally associated with dietary deficiency experienced on the high seas. Having said that, their diet did include the familiar seafarer's staples of salted meat or fish plus the dreaded ship's biscuit. From evidence recovered from the wreck it is clear that these were at least sometimes supplemented with meat and fruit. Several barrels were found to contain bones of venison, mutton and

◄ The wooden log reel which would have been used to unravel a knotted line into the water to establish the ship's speed.

...began to enjoy a growth in luxury and increase in comfort. Working people like the barber-surgeon and carpenter became wealthier, using their skills to improve their position in Tudor society.

2

"Such furniture of householde of this mettall as we commaunt, vyz to the value of oecxxli is sould asually by the garnish which doth contayn pewter platters, twelve dishes, and twelve saucers..."

Stamped with the letters GC, these 11 dishes, 9 plates and 8 saucers may represent the remains of a garnish (dinner set) owned by Sir George Carew, Lord Lisle's Vice Admiral on board the *Mary Rose*.

However, in the final analysis, the ownership of pewter was dependent on one thing - money. Without it a person owned nothing. The truest sign of wealth amo...

This copper flagon, with its foot, was used to serve wine.

These pewter flasks and...found in the barber-surgeon's...have been used to store big precious dry powders.

When this object was unearthed have been used as a "pomander" (self-bellied) ...minister. Pomander was used to measure out m...

pork, possibly from smoked or salted cuts of meat. The remains of headless fish were also discovered in a basket. In general the crew were better fed than their counterparts on dry land. Regulations from 1565, only twenty years after the *Mary Rose* was lost, stipulated that each crewman had a weekly allowance of seven pounds of biscuit, seven gallons of beer – this was the standard drink as the stored water was not usually fit for consumption – eight pounds of salt beef, three quarters of a pound of fish, three eighths of a pound of butter and three fifths of a pound of cheese.

The food was cooked in the 'kychen' or galley located in the hold at the bottom of the ship. A firebox consisting of 4,000 bricks supported two large cauldrons which would have been used to turn most of the ingredients into stews. A smaller pot was used to prepare meals for the officers who would have dined from pewter plates or dishes, with pewter tankards and spoons while the rest of the crew had wooden ones. Hundreds of these were recovered from the wreck with many of them displaying their owner's mark.

CLOTHING

There was no official uniform for the men serving on the king's ships, but there are references in the royal wardrobe to coats of green and white being supplied to soldiers on the *Mary Rose*, although these might have been for purely ceremonial purposes. In general, few examples of ordinary clothing have survived from Tudor times and in this instance the *Mary Rose* time capsule has little to offer as only the leather goods survived; woollen or linen garments

◀ A large selection of pewter dishes, jugs and containers brought to the surface after almost 450 years on the seabed.

A leather jerkin which was stitched together with silk thread. The bodice is pinked and snipped in an elaborate all-over design. It may have been worn by an archer as it was found associated with archery equipment.

have mostly perished, with the exception of a handful of items including velvet and woollen hats. There are examples of leather clothing on display at the Mary Rose Museum in Portsmouth and the largest of these is a leather jerkin, a type of sleeveless jacket or waistcoat. Other examples in the collection are decorated with pinking and slashing. One features bound edges and a leather roll around the arm holes. The other leather items to be found in large quantities were shoes in a variety of styles and also long boots.

◄◄ *A fine example of a preserved leather jerkin, a sort of sleeveless garment with a short skirt or lower flap. This may have been worn by an archer.*

◄ *A representation of a typical jerkin of the period.*

TOOLS

It was essential to make running repairs to the wooden ship and various objects while at sea, which is why so many tools have been recovered including a range of essential carpentry tools such as mallets, braces to drill holes, planes and mortice gauges. A grindstone was used to keep the tools and knives sharp. One of the biggest surprises to emerge from the wreck was the presence of shot moulds and ingots of lead which indicate that shot was actually being cast on the ship.

Shoes and clothing were repaired on board too. Ribbon, thread, buttons, pins and thimbles have been found, as well as a simple weaving loom which was probably used to make basic items such as strops for the equipment.

It was important that day-to-day repairs could be carried out on board. These wood-working tools recovered from the carpenter's cabin would be readily identified by his modern counterparts. (The Mary Rose Trust)

Carpenters at work using similar hand tools to those recovered from the wreck.

ENTERTAINMENTS

A number of musical instruments were discovered on the *Mary Rose*, although it is not known whether these were personal possessions or belonged to an official band of some sort. In Elizabethan times it was not unusual to have professional musicians on board. A tabor drum and three tabor pipes were found in the crew's quarters. These were played together as a sort of one-man band, with the melody played on the pipes in one hand while the other hand beat out the rhythm on the drum. Other instruments include a unique example of a shawm or douçaine, a type of oboe which disappeared from the musical scene during the sixteenth century, plus fragments from two Tudor fiddles which consisted of simple

◄ *One of the many clay pots recovered from the* Mary Rose.

◀ *This display depicts two of the musical instruments recovered from the Mary Rose. The douçaine or still shawm, on the left, is an oboe-like instrument, while the man on the right plays a fiddle.*

▶ *Detail of the still shawm and beneath it a modern replica.*

Did you know?

The term knot, meaning a speed of 1 nautical mile per hour, comes from the knotted rope which mariners used to estimate their speed. A nautical mile is one minute of arc of a degree of latitude, which is roughly 1.15 statute miles.

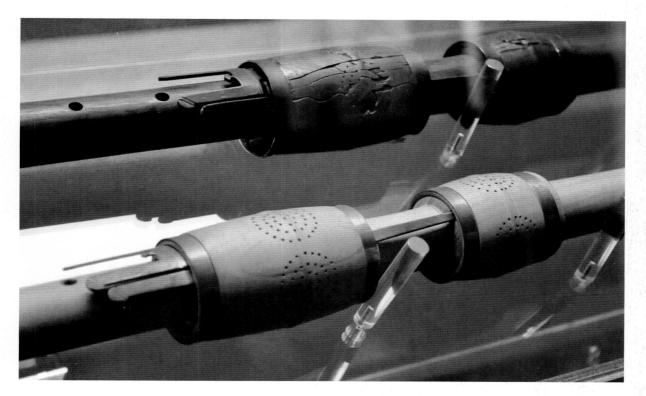

rectangular sound boards with straight necks rather than the more elaborately shaped instrument we know today.

A number of recreational items were recovered including a very fine backgammon board, complete with its counters, located in a cabin used by the ship's carpenter. Several dice made of bone were also found. The remnants of leather book covers as well as quills and ink pots indicate that the senior officers, at least, would have been educated and literate men.

◀◀ *A sixteenth-century tabor player with a drum to strike the beat and a pipe to play the melody.*

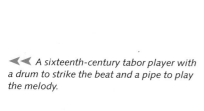

◀ *Easily recognised, a wooden backgammon board and counters.*

▲ *The remains of a leather book binding. Only the officers would have been literate and many personal objects on board the ship would have been identified by an owner's mark.*

Oh, my gallant men! Oh, my gallant men!

Henry VIII upon witnessing the sinking of the *Mary Rose*, 19 July 1545

Our galleys had all the advantages of working which we could desire to the great damage of the English who for want of wind not being able to stir laid exposed to our cannon …

D'Annebault, French Admiral at the Battle of the Solent, 1545

On Saturday 18 July 1545 the French invasion fleet, estimated at anything between 123 and 300 strong but mostly likely around the 200 mark, including a number of oar-powered galleys, dropped anchor off the eastern entrance to the Solent. In command was Admiral D'Annebault. Inexperienced in naval matters, he nonetheless held a considerable advantage in comparison with the English admiral, John Dudley, Viscount Lisle, who had only eighty or so ships at his disposal. The English fleet was gathered in Portsmouth and although anticipated reinforcements from the West Country and the Thames had not arrived, Lisle's fleet still held a strong defensive position in the restricted waters of the Solent. In particular the experienced English mariners could navigate safely between the sandbanks on either even though the marker buoys had been removed or repositioned to confound the enemy. And if the French ships did manage to navigate up the water channel they would be well within the range of the gun batteries at Southsea Castle and the other gun towers.

➤ *A clash of galleys in the Mediterranean. These oar-powered row-barges were ideally suited to shallower inland waters or in conditions when sail-powered vessels were becalmed.*

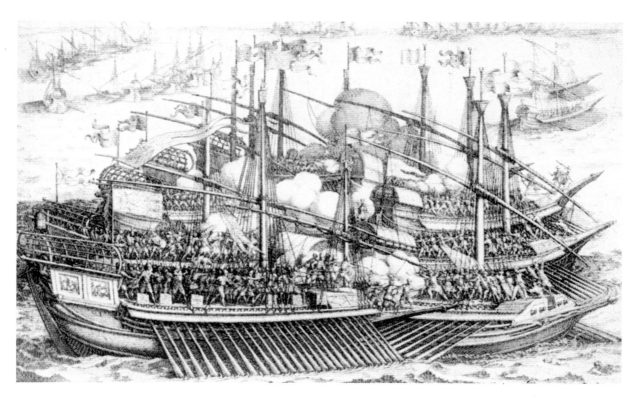

As with the Mary Rose, the Great Harry is depicted on the Anthony Roll with several rows of gunports plus rear-facing guns at the stern.

The first day of what became known as the Battle of the Solent consisted of an exploratory long-range cannonade between the French galleys, which were ideally suited to the shallow waters, and the English ships, but without any significant damage. The French also put troops ashore on the Isle of Wight where they tangled with the local militia. In Portsmouth the morale of the English was boosted by the presence of Henry VIII who, as Commander-in-Chief, had set up camp beside Southsea Castle with an army of 12,000 men. On that evening, 18 October, he dined on the flagship, *Henry Grace à Dieu*, to discuss strategies and issue orders to his senior naval officers including Dudley and the newly appointed vice-admiral, Sir George Carew, who would be on the *Mary Rose* during the following day's engagement.

The morning of Sunday 19 July dawned clear and bright with scarcely a breath of wind. Many of the details concerning events on that fateful day are largely conjectural because the accounts that have been passed down to us vary in their detail and there is little hard evidence to go on. It appears that Henry was aboard the *Henry Grace à Dieu* once again and had just finished eating when a lookout spotted the sails of the French fleet. As his officers returned to their ships, the king was taken ashore and took up a position on the castle ramparts where he was joined by Sir George Carew's wife, Lady Mary, and several others. From there he had an unimpeded view as the opposing ships gathered like the pieces in an elaborate chess game.

In the calm conditions the French pushed their galleys forward and fired at the English ships with impunity, goading them into joining the battle. At first the crews of the English warships struggled to make headway, but by late afternoon the wind picked up a little with the ebbing tide and at last the sails could be hoisted and set. It was a scene of utter confusion in the narrow channel of water between the sandbanks with the crews manoeuvring their ships tightly as they avoided colliding or tangling their rigging as they worked towards the open waters. Two of the larger ships, the *Henry Grace à Dieu* and the *Mary Rose*, still considered one of the most nimble warships in the fleet, broke away from the pack to attack the French galleys. The *Mary Rose* is said to have taken the lead and with her sails catching the

> *During the Battle of the Solent the king watched in horror from the shore as the Mary Rose heeled over and sank.*

freshening breeze the *Mary Rose* began to heel over. When roughly halfway between Southsea Castle and Ryde Sands she fired a broadside and then started to come about to bring the guns on the other side to bear upon the enemy vessels. Suddenly she leaned heavily towards the starboard side and the water rushed in through the lower gunports which had been left open after firing.

As the ship lurched to one side the level decks became treacherous slopes with equipment, ammunition, supplies and crewmen thrown into one chaotic tumble. One of the heavy guns broke loose. Below decks the brick oven in the galley collapsed and was thrown across the ship. It is possible that the ballast in the hold had shifted, although whether this caused the sinking or happened afterwards is uncertain. We do

know that the companionways connecting the decks, and also the doorways, became tightly jammed bottlenecks for the seamen desperately trying to escape, as indicated by the position of skeletons found on the wreck. It was no better on the upper decks where anti-boarding netting prevented escape. The men were trapped on their own ship like fish in a net, their cries heard from the shore, clutching at the daylight as the cold water engulfed them. The sinking of the *Mary Rose* was as rapid as it was unexpected, but for the poor souls on board those few moments of turmoil must have been an eternity. On the shore the king watched in horror as the tragedy unfolded before his eyes. He gave a gasp of utter dismay. 'Oh, my gallant gentlemen! Oh, my gallant gentlemen!'

◄ Sir George Carew was in command of the Mary Rose *when she sank in the Solent on 19 July 1545. Portrait by Hans Holbein the Younger.*

The ship had sunk in only 45ft (14m) of water. The 'Cowdry Picture', painted in 1545 (and destroyed by fire in 1793), is the only contemporary depiction of the last moments of the *Mary Rose* and it shows just the tips of her masts breaking the surface of the water. No one is sure exactly how many people were aboard when she went down. Some estimates suggest as

◄◄ *The Cowdry Engraving is based on a lost painting which showed the moment when the* Mary Rose *sank. The French galleys are to the left and the English fleet to the right; the top of the masts of the* Mary Rose *are visible above Southsea Castle.*

◄ *The skeleton of a dog which was recovered near the doorway of the carpenter's cabin. She was probably on board as a mascot or pet and would have been put to work dealing with the rats.*

Did you know?

A morris pike was a wooden staff of between 16 and 20ft in length with a very sharp point at the tip. The word morris is a corruption of Moorish.

many as 700 while most historians put the figure at nearer 400. With the exception of some men stationed in the top mast, almost all of the crew perished including Sir George Carew and Roger Grenville. In total fewer than forty men survived.

WHY DID THE *MARY ROSE* SINK?

The cause of the sinking has been the subject of much speculation over the years. Not surprisingly the French claim that they had sunk the *Mary Rose*, but the actual explanation probably lies in a number of contributing factors with the open gunports being the prime suspects. The eighteenth-century naval historian Josiah Burchett asserted that the lower ones were only 16in (40.6cm) above the water line. However, this figure has been largely discredited; as Stuart Vine of the Mary Rose Trust says, 'If this had been the case the *Mary Rose* would never have left port.' He believes that they must have been closer to 4ft (1.2m) from the water. Maritime archaeologist Peter Marsden asserts that the modifications to the *Mary Rose*, particularly the weight of the additional heavy guns, may have brought them lower. He also suggests that the guns had not been fired and the ship was simply turning sharply to avoid the Ryde sandbank. But surely a competent crew would have taken steps to ensure that the gunports were properly closed in such a manoeuvre? Sir Peter Carew, the brother of Sir George Carew, gave an eyewitness account of the sinking to his biographer, John Hooker, in 1857. He reports that their uncle, Sir Gawain Carew, had sailed close to the *Mary Rose* and he had asked Sir George why the ship was heeling when the sails were raised:

This gentleman ... had in his ship a hundred mariners, the worst of them being able to be a master in the best ship in the realm; and these so maligned and disdained one another, that refusing to do that which they should do, were careless to that which was most needful ...

Put all of these factors together and we have a ship that had a tendency to heel in sail, with open gunports which at best were only a few feet from the water line, compounded by a crew that neglected to carry out essential tasks.

A person equipped in this apparatus being enabled to descend to considerable depths, from 20 fathoms (120ft) to probably 30 fathoms (180ft) and to remain down several hours having the perfect use of his arms and legs and is freely able to traverse the bottom of the sea to seek out the hidden treasures of the deep.

John Deane, instructions on using diving helmet

The tragic loss of the *Mary Rose* and most of her crew did not, in itself, bring an end to the Battle of the Solent. Certainly the English admiral, John Dudley, had lost one of the two most important ships in his fleet and, along with it, a significant share of his available firepower, but the battle wore on for two more days. While the English seamen reeled from the shock of the sinking, the French, not unreasonably thinking that they had been responsible, were keen to push home their advantage. However, the fickle winds on the evening of 19 July 1545 once again fell calm and accordingly the French withdrew their galleys. For most of the following day, Monday 20 July, the engagement continued with both sides exchanging cannon fire, and then, on the Tuesday, Admiral D'Annebault attempted to draw Dudley into battle by putting soldiers ashore on the Isle of Wight where they set several houses alight. Dudley, however, was having none of it and by all accounts the local garrison and the islanders put up enough of a fight to send the French running 'like hares' back to their ships. Frustrated by the weather and Dudley's reluctance to engage more fully, the French invasion fleet withdrew.

The impact that the sinking of the *Mary Rose* must have had upon the English, especially the superstitious sailors who most probably saw it as God's will, is inestimable. Raising the ship was a priority, not only to lift morale but also to restore the fleet to its full strength. This was standard practice as a warship was an expensive commodity and building a replacement would inevitably take some time. Only days after the sinking the Secretary of State, William Paget, ordered a salvage and the king's brother-in-law, Charles Brandon, was put in charge of the arrangements. He immediately hired a Venetian salvage team consisting of thirty-one men, and he put together a detailed list of the equipment they would need. The plan was to position two hulks or empty ships on the surface at low tide to either side of the wreck. The two ships to be used were *Jesus of Lubeck* and the *Samson*, each of 700 tons 'burthen' or burden. Strong cables lowered from the hulks would be attached to the wreck, usually by passing them under or around the hull itself, and if all went well it would be lifted or 'weighed' at high tide and moved to shallower waters where the process would be repeated until it was on sufficiently high ground to be pumped out.

On 1 August 1545 Brandon wrote to the king in confident mood:

I trust by Monday or Tuesday at the furthest the Mary Rose shall be weighed up and saved. There be two hulkes, cables, pulleys and other things made ready …

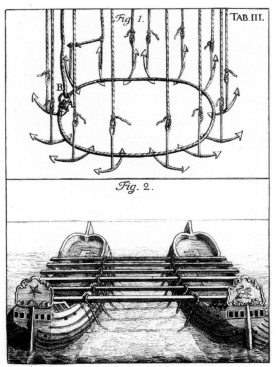

TAB. III.

Fig. 1.

Fig. 2.

But his confidence proved to be unfounded. When the *Mary Rose* sunk her hull had settled on the seabed at an angle of 60 degrees to starboard and at a right angle against the currents of the Solent, albeit at a depth of only 45ft (14m) or so. The tilt was not a particular problem, but when the hull had come to rest it had broken through the soft upper sediments and because of the angle a large surface area was in contact with the clay below. This would not only require a far greater lifting power to pull it free, it also made it impossible to pass the cables underneath the hull. The Venetians attempted to right the hull by attaching cables to the main mast, but they only succeeded in tearing it out of the mast-step in the keelson. The ship wouldn't budge and over the following years several guns and other items were raised from the

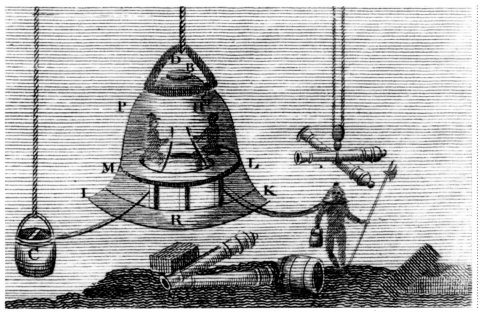

◄◄ The traditional method of raising a wreck was to place two hulks on either side and lift it with the tide and move to shallower waters. This process would be repeated in stages until the ship was exposed at low tide and could be pumped out.

◄ In 1691 Edmund Halley devised his diving bell and this diagram also shows a smaller version being used as a helmet.

wreck. Even so, right up until Henry VIII's death in January 1547, or possibly even later, there remained a lingering hope that the ship might yet be raised.

Over the next 200 years the *Mary Rose* gradually faded from memory, although it is said that the wreck remained visible at low tide until the late sixteenth century. On the seabed the tides carved two scour pits or ditches on either side of those parts of the wreck which were mostly buried in the clay, while the abrasive action of the sand and silt carried in the currents, aided by bacteria and wood-boring creatures, weakened the exposed timber structure until it collapsed upon itself or was washed away. What remained of the hull, thought to be around 40 per cent, was gradually covered by layers of sediment and a protective layer of compacted clay and crushed shells, with the shifting tides and currents occasionally exposing some timbers.

REDISCOVERY

In June 1836 a fisherman's net happened to catch on the end of one of these timbers. By chance a professional diver named John Deane was working on the wreck of the *Royal George*, less than a mile (1km) to the south-west. This was a 100-gun first-rate ship of the line, built at Woolwich Dockyard and launched in 1756. In a curious parallel with the earlier sinking of the *Mary Rose*, the *Royal George* had sunk when water entered its lower gunports. On the morning of 28 August 1782 the ship was at anchor at Spithead at Portsmouth, her decks packed with visitors as she was due to depart for Gibraltar very shortly, and a large workforce of men on board carrying out maintenance on her hull. In order to roll her over slightly in the water, orders were given for the guns on one side of the ship to be moved to the centreline. Unfortunately she heeled over too far and water rushed in through the gunports, left open to allow for the loading of rum barrels, sinking the ship and drowning around 650 of the 900 people on board.

John Deane, together with his brother Charles, had originally patented their 'Smoke Helmet' in 1823 as an aid in fighting fires in the hold of ships. It consisted of a copper helmet with an attached flexible collar and garment, with a long hose going from the rear to a pump which supplied the fresh air. When commercial interest in the smoke helmet apparatus proved elusive the brothers converted it into a diving helmet and suit, and it became of the forerunner

➤ *The diving suit made underwater work routine. This engraving of divers investigating the wreck of the Northfleet was published in* The Illustrated London News *in 1873.*

➤➤ *Early twentieth-century divers with a conventional suit beside a special deep-water suit developed by Jim Jarret to explore the wreck of the* Lusitania *in 1935. (NOAA)*

➤ *A Victorian deep-sea diver with diving suit, a direct descendant of Deane's designs.*

of all diving suits ever since. Alerted by the fishermen, John Deane made a series of dives on the *Mary Rose* in 1836 and again in 1840, and they recovered a number of objects including timbers, bronze and iron guns, as well as longbows and other objects. The inscriptions on the guns led the wreck to being identified as Henry

Did you know?

Larboard used to be the term for the left side of a ship when looking forward, but it was changed to 'port' to avoid confusion with 'starboard', on the right, when giving orders.

VIII's lost warship. Driven by widespread interest in the discovery and the high prices commanded by recovered relics, Deane resorted to using explosive charges to blast his way into parts of the ship. Similar methods were frequently used to clear wrecks obstructing the passage of ships through the Solent and the remains of the *Royal George* were disposed of in this way. By good fortune Deane never penetrated the main surviving section of the *Mary Rose* which was protected and concealed beneath the hard crust.

▲ *Two of the iron guns recovered from the* Mary Rose *by Charles Deane. (J.&C. McCutcheon Collection)*

As we came through the harbour entrance we became aware that the ancient walls built by the Tudor kings to defend Portsmouth were alive with a seething mass of people. We shouted at them and they cheered us and the cheers rose to a crescendo as the *Mary Rose* entered harbour. What a moment!

Margaret Rule on the return of the *Mary Rose*, 11 October 1982

The quest to locate the forgotten wreck of the *Mary Rose* in modern times was driven by the dedication of journalist and amateur diver Alexander McKee. In 1965, together with the Southsea branch of the British Sub-Aqua Club, he initiated a project to locate a number of shipwrecks in the Solent, including the *Mary Rose*. By this time the upper part of the wreck, the port side, had been weakened, eroded and washed away, but a major part of the starboard side of the ship was embedded in soft sediments, sealed in by a hard layer of shelly clay. An old chart from 1841 indicated the position of the wreck reasonably accurately and this coincided with a trench, scoured out by the tides, at the dive site. In 1967 sonar scanning equipment revealed a sub-seabed anomaly, an oval feature about 200ft (61m) long and McKee knew that he had found the *Mary Rose*. Over the next few years the investigative dives continued. In 1970 a loose timber was located and the following spring some structural details were identified after they had been partially uncovered by

A row of cast bronze guns on display at the Mary Rose Museum in Portsmouth.

One of the last objects to be recovered from the seabed was the ship's bronze bell. The writing in Flemish translates as, 'I have been cast in 1510.'

winter storms. Clearly this was a site of some archaeological significance and in order to protect the wreck from plunderers the newly formed Mary Rose Committee arranged to lease a section of the seabed from the Portsmouth authorities for the princely sum of £1 per year.

The rediscovery of the wreck began to attract increasing media and public attention, especially when the project received royal patronage from Prince Charles who took a keen interest and later participated in several dives on the site. By 1974 the committee had become a registered charity with the aim of not only excavating the wreck, but also recovering and preserving the remains of the hull. It would be a hugely complex and expensive task, but it was not without precedent. The *Vasa* was a Swedish warship, built

◄ *Ship's blocks and pulleys on display at the Mary Rose Museum.*

Did you know?
As only the educated members of the crew could read, personal possessions had identification marks to denote ownership, and important parts of the ship such as hatches and their covers were also clearly marked in this way.

◄ *The Tudor rose on one of the cast bronze guns.*

► *The* Mary Rose *has a counterpart in the* Vasa, *a Swedish ship which sank on its first voyage in 1828 and was recovered from Stockholm harbour in the 1960s. (Peter Isotalo)*

A scale model of the lifting frame or cradle in which the Mary Rose was raised to the surface in 1982.

A tense moment on the morning of 11 October 1982. The lifting frame and cradle are just below the surface prior to the final lift. (The Mary Rose Trust)

around 1626, which foundered and sank after sailing just over a mile (1.8km) into its maiden voyage. The ship had toppled over because it was top heavy and lacked sufficient ballast. Once the bronze cannon had been salvaged the wreck was largely

99

forgotten until rediscovered in the 1950s lying beneath a busy shipping lane in Stockholm harbour. Unlike the *Mary Rose* the *Vasa's* hull was largely intact and rested upright on the seabed. It was successfully raised in 1961 and over the next seventeen years the hull was sprayed with polyethylene glycol to preserve the timbers and then slow dried for another nine years. It is now the centrepiece of the Vasa Museum in Stockholm which opened in 1990.

Raising the delicate remains of the *Mary Rose* was going to be far more difficult and there was no guarantee that it would survive being lifted by conventional methods using cables slung under the hull, much as they did in Tudor times, or with buoyancy devices. In 1980 it was decided that the hull would be excavated, emptied of its contents, and then strengthened with steel braces and suspended beneath a lifting frame to be raised from the seabed and placed on a purpose-built support cradle before being lifted out of the water. With concerns about further erosion to the wreck the deadline for the lift was set for 1982. The scale of the colossal excavation operation needed to prepare the hull is revealed in the statistics: A team headed by marine archaeologist Margaret Rule carried out a total of 27,831 dives between 1979 and 1982, excavating the wreck and bringing 2,895 timbers and 20,571 artefacts to the surface. The next task was to raise the ship itself.

The morning of 11 October 1982 dawned clear with calm conditions. In the Solent a flotilla of small boats, packed with the media and spectators including Prince

◀ *The moment when the remains of the* Mary Rose *were hoisted out of the water. (The Mary Rose Trust)*

Charles, gathered around the lifting barge *Tog Mor* which towered above the wreck site like a huge praying mantis. Very slowly it began to raise the frame and its precious cargo out of the murky waters and millions more people watched the live television broadcast as the yellow frame broke the surface. Shortly afterwards the cradle holding the remains of the *Mary Rose* emerged into the daylight when, suddenly, a retaining pin on one of the supporting legs of the framework snapped. The frame lurched down on one side by about 3ft (1m) with a crunch, threatening to crush the fragile hull. It was a heart-stopping moment, but fortunately no damage had been done and by late afternoon the *Tog Mor* had successfully lowered the cradle on to the barge *Tow One*. With the weather deteriorating it was impossible to remove the lifting frame safely on site and the whole 570-ton package was towed into Portsmouth harbour. The *Mary Rose* had finally come home after 437 years on the seabed.

The result of all this hard work and expertise is that future generations, we hope, will be able to glimpse a small part of Britain's maritime heritage; will be able to see history come alive …

HRH Prince Charles – Foreword to *The Mary Rose*, 1982

The next stage in saving the *Mary Rose* was going to be a two-part operation: one to protect and preserve the fabric of the hull and its timbers, the other to save the thousands of artefacts which had been brought to the surface during the dives.

Following the raising of the wreck on 11 October 1982, one of the first tasks was to carefully move the lifting frame out of the way, leaving the hull on its support cradle and lying at the same 60-degree angle as it had rested on the seabed. With the timber exposed to the air for the first time after more than 400 years under water, it was essential to prevent it from drying out too quickly. Without appropriate conservation the waterlogged timber could have shrunk by as much as 20-50 per cent, resulting in severe cracking and warping as the water evaporated from the cellular structure of the wood. The hull was protected with layers of expanded foam and on 8 December 1982 moved into No.3 dock, almost within the shadow of HMS *Victory*. By the following year a lightweight aluminium roof structure, double skinned and insulated, covered the dry dock to create a temporary ship hall. A new spray system was installed and the hull was constantly sprayed with water

➤ A selection of the 170 longbows recovered from the wreck.

➤➤ The remains of the starboard section of the Mary Rose *undergoing conservation in a mist of polyethylene glycol. (The Mary Rose Trust)*

chilled to 5°C to keep it from drying out and to inhibit fungi or bacterial growth on the timbers. In 1985 the ship was turned upright and titanium rods were installed to support the internal structure, and, aided by the highly detailed drawings prepared during the underwater excavations, it was possible to start reinstating the deck timbers.

The *Mary Rose* conservation team was fortunate in being able to draw upon the experience of conservationists working on the recovered hull of the *Vasa* in Stockholm, and after ten years of small-scale trials, a three-phase conservation programme was instigated in 1994. During the first phase, lasting twelve years, the hull was sprayed with a solution of low-molecular-weight polyethylene glycol (PEG). This waxy substance gradually replaced the water

content in the timbers. Then a thicker, hotter mix was introduced in 2004 to coat and seal the outer layers of the timbers. The spraying process was completed in 2010; the ship is now undergoing the final phase, controlled air drying, scheduled to continue until 2016 (*see* Chapter 10, The Final Voyage).

In 2002 the Ministry of Defence informed the Mary Rose Trust that it intended enlarging the approach into Portsmouth harbour, in order to accommodate new aircraft carriers, and this would entail dredging a channel through the eastern corner of the wreck site. A new phase of intensive underwater archaeology began in 2003 with the aim of recovering any objects left behind from the 1979–1982 excavations and finding objects left buried in the seabed outside of the hull. The dives continued until 2005 and as well as finding a quantity of smaller objects, including coins and weapons, there were several larger finds. These included a 32.8ft (10m) long piece of the stempost, the forward extension of the keel which rises up in a curve at the front of the ship to form the bow, and one of the ship's anchors.

The MoD has since changed its plans to dredge through the site and although the latest phase of underwater excavation has come to a close, there are sure to be more finds in the future. The site is protected by the 1973 Protection of Wrecks Act, and diving can only be carried out under a licence issued by the Secretary of State for Culture, Media and Sport which is currently held by a member of the Mary Rose Trust. The wreck site is also monitored annually.

◄ A protective suit protects a conservation worker from the polyethylene glycol spray. The spraying phase of the conservation process was completed in 2010.

CONSERVING THE ARTEFACTS

Just as with the ship's timbers, the thousands of artefacts also needed to be conserved. The variety of objects and the range of different materials would present their own particular challenges. Most of these artefacts, from the huge cannon to small personal objects, had been brought to the surface during the initial excavation of the ship between 1979 and 1982. Each

Did you know?

'Swinging the lead' refers to the lead-weighted line lowered over the side of a ship to determine depth in shallow waters. Sometimes the weight had soft wax on the underside to take a sample of the seabed.

One of the wooden gunshields after conservation. The individual wooden objects were treated in a similar way to the ship's timbers.

one was carefully catalogued and recorded by finds assistants on the diving vessel Sleipner before being brought ashore. Most of the wooden objects were treated with polyethylene glycol, as with the hull, then freeze-dried and the water content removed under vacuum followed by controlled air drying. More hardy materials, such as the bricks from the galley oven, were washed free of salt and allowed to air-dry.

The method of conserving metal objects varies. Alloys of lead and pewter, which accounted for hundreds of the everyday utensils such as bowls, dishes and jugs, are inherently stable, only requiring careful washing and a coating of protective wax. Iron, copper and copper alloy objects were kept moist in a sodium sesquicarbonate solution to prevent oxidisation in the atmosphere or a reaction with chlorides that had permeated their surface during the prolonged immersion in salt water. Iron and steel objects, such as swords or knife blades, had suffered particularly badly underwater. In one case all that remained of a sword was a shadow caused by the corroding steel staining the sediment.

More delicate objects, especially those made from organic materials such as leather or fabric, required very careful handling. This applied in particular to examples of clothing and one of the most delicate artefacts was the barber-surgeon's silk velvet cap. All items of clothing were recorded in detail before the conservation process began and polythene patterns were

▲ *Pewter and pewter-alloy objects, such as this dish, survived their long immersion surprisingly well.*

◄ *A wooden bucket after conservation.* (The Mary Rose Trust)

◄ Small metalware flasks and jugs.

➤ An assortment of clay and wooden pots and containers, some from the barber-surgeon's chest.

The handles from razors, minus the blades which had corroded away in the seawater.

made as a guide to how the garments fitted together. In many cases this enabled the conservators to create replicas which in turn provided accurate indications of the stature of individual crew members. All of the *Mary Rose* artefacts are kept in a closely controlled environment, including those on display in the museum, to protect them from fluctuations in humidity and temperature and to ensure that this unique Tudor time capsule survives for future generations to appreciate.

A thigh-length leather boot, probably belonging to one of the officers. It is quite probable that many of the ordinary crew went barefoot.

There is still much to do, but the support of the public and the enthusiasm of young visitors encourages us to believe that, in the case of the Mary Rose, there is a future for the past.

Mary Rose Trust

Once the *Mary Rose* and her contents had been safely brought ashore the Trust then had to decide how best to display their Tudor treasures. Originally they proposed building a Tudor Ship museum on the eastern end of Portsea Island at Eastney, but this plan was put on hold in 1982 because of the need to prioritise all efforts on the conservation work. At that time the future of the Royal Naval base at Portsmouth was far from certain, but the presence of HMS *Victory* and the freeing up of other dock buildings saw a large area gradually transformed into the Portsmouth Historic Dockyard as a popular visitor attraction. The nineteenth-century iron-hulled warship, *Warrior*, arrived there in June 1987 and was later joined by the *M33*, an M29-class monitor, a class of small warship built in 1915 and one of only two surviving First World War ships. Now that the dock had four historic warships to attract visitors, and with work continuing on preserving the *Mary Rose*, in 1984 a temporary *Mary Rose* exhibition was established in No.5 Boathouse, near to the dockyard entrance. Here visitors could see a selection of the recovered artefacts before viewing the ship in the dry dock, peering in through protective windows at the dark

➤ *The new Mary Rose Museum taking shape alongside Nelson's flagship HMS* Victory, *photographed in 2011.*

timbers which were usually shrouded in a mist of chemical sprays. With this wet phase of the conservation completed in 2010, the trust finally saw the opportunity to reunite ship and contents in a single purpose-built museum.

The new museum will be constructed around the ship which will remain in situ within its dock and will not be moved from its cradle. As you would expect, the design of the building is very modern, shaped like an oval clad in wood with clean lines that

➤ *One of the major difficulties facing the architects and builders is in erecting the new structure in situ around the dry dock containing the* Mary Rose.

mimic the shape of the dry dock and echo traditional boat construction. John Lippiet, Chief Executive of the Mary Rose Trust, is well aware of the practical difficulties in building the new museum around the ship:

It is a huge challenge to build safely not only over a unique 450-year-old structure but also on a site which is in itself a Scheduled Ancient Monument. But we have a team which has developed a scheme that manages to be both stunning and subtle. It is hugely sympathetic to its dockyard surroundings and at the same time highly practical for our unique needs.

Architects Wilkson Eyre have described the new museum as an elliptical 'jewel box' which will have the hull at its centre with

When completed, the new museum will provide the opportunity to display the objects beside the ship.

Did you know?
Sailors customarily drank beer as water did not store well. In 1565 the allowance for each man was seven gallons of beer a week; that's a gallon a day. Even so, drunkenness on duty was a punishable offence.

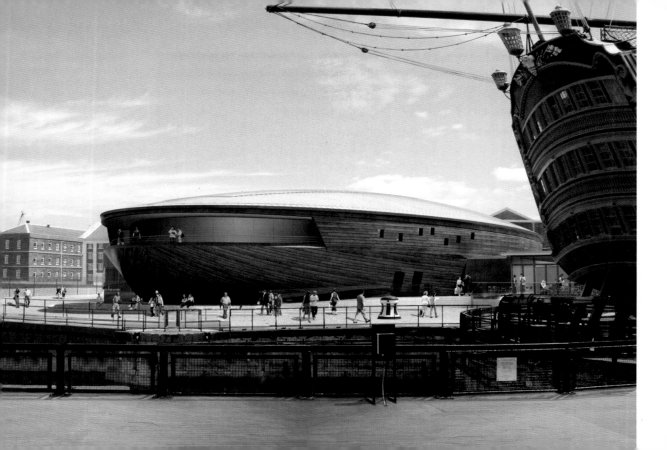

galleries running the length of the ship, each at a level corresponding to the deck levels of the ship, where the artefacts will be displayed. One of the benefits of the new building is that they can display 60 per cent of the collection, and many items will be seen by the public for the first time.

Salvaging and conserving the *Mary Rose* has been one of the most ambitious and significant heritage projects in recent years and inevitably this latest phase will be a massively expensive one. The Heritage Lottery Fund has stepped in with £21 million leaving the Mary Rose Trust to raise the remaining £15 million. In September 2009 the temporary display hall housing the hull was closed to the public to allow construction work to commence. However, the display in No.5 Boathouse remains on view until the new Mary Rose Museum is completed in the autumn of 2012, thirty years after the Tudor warship was brought to the surface. For the first four years the hull will remain in what they are calling the 'hotbox', the chamber in which it will be carefully dried out to remove the tons of water the timbers now contain. Visitors will be able to view the hull through large observation windows on each gallery level and they will see the temporary air ducts running through the decks. This drying process should be completed in 2016 when the ducts and hotbox will be removed to reveal the hull in its entirety. At that point the *Mary Rose* will become more than just a time capsule; it will become a time machine through which visitors can travel back 500 years.

◀ The architects Wilkinson Eyre have created an elliptical wooden 'jewel box' placing the hull of the Mary Rose at its centre with galleries running the length of the ship. It is due to open in 2012. (The Mary Rose Trust)

APPENDIX 1 – TIMELINE

1509	21 April: Henry VIII becomes king at the age of seventeen.
1510	Construction of the *Mary Rose* commences in Portsmouth.
1511	July: The *Mary Rose* is launched.
1512	*Mary Rose* is involved in battle with the Spanish against the French in the English Channel.
1522	England is again at war with France. The *Mary Rose* participates in the escort to the transport of troops.
1522–1545	The ship is kept in reserve.
1536	The *Mary Rose* is rebuilt and upgraded from 500 to 700 tons.
1545	19 July: The *Mary Rose* sinks in full sight of the king during the Battle of the Solent.
1547	28 January: The death of Henry VIII at the age of fifty-five.
1836	After fishermen catch their nets in the wreck, pioneering divers John and Charles Deane investigate the site and recover a bronze demi cannon gun.
1971	5 May: The first structural details of the wreck are identified.
1973	Passing of the Protection of Wrecks Act.
1979	Mary Rose Trust is formed with HRH Prince Charles as its president.
1982	11 October: The wreck of the *Mary Rose* is raised from the seabed.

1984	9 July: Opening of The Mary Rose Museum at Portsmouth's Historic Dockyard.
2003	A new phase of underwater archaeology is carried out after the MoD announces it needs to improve access to Portsmouth harbour for its aircraft carriers.
2010	The spraying process is finally completed and the hull begins a five-year period of controlled air drying.
2011	500th anniversary of the ship's launch. The Royal Mint issues a special commemorative £2 coin to mark the occasion.

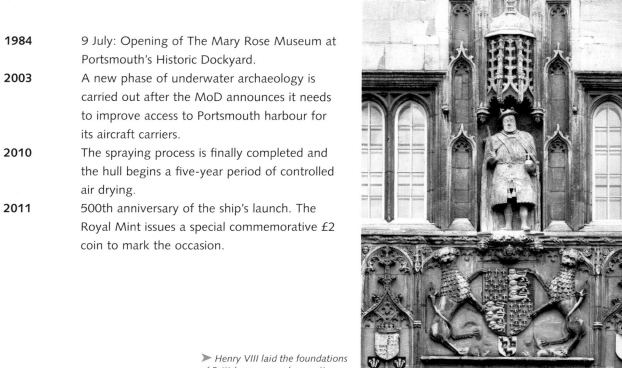

➤ *Henry VIII laid the foundations of British sea power by creating what would become the Royal Navy. (Andreas Praefcke)*

APPENDIX 2 – PLACES TO VISIT

The *Mary Rose* and the Portsmouth Historic Dockyard

Hampshire: The obvious place to start. See not only the *Mary Rose* and the new museum, which is due to open in 2012, but also the National Museum of the Royal Navy, HMS *Victory* plus the 1860 HMS *Warrior*, the world's first iron-hulled battleship.

www.maryrose.org

www.historicdockyard.co.uk

Southsea Castle

Hampshire: The castle in Portsmouth, built as part of a series of fortifications constructed by Henry VIII to protect the south coast. It was from here that the king witnessed the sinking of the *Mary Rose*.

www.southseacastle.co.uk

The National Maritime Museum

Greenwich, London: The world's largest maritime museum.

www.nmm.ac.uk

The Vasa Museum

Djurgarden, Stockholm: This Swedish warship sank in 1628 and was salvaged in 1961.

www.vasamuseet.se/en

➤ *Admiral Lord Nelson's famous flagship HMS* Victory *at Portsmouth's historic dockyard.*

➤ The nineteenth-century ironclad Warrior, *now moored at Portsmouth.*

➤➤ *One of only two surviving ships from the First World War, the M33 Monitor is in a dry dock near to the* Mary Rose *and HMS* Victory.

Spitbank Fort is one of a series of sea-based forts constructed between 1861 and 1878 to repel French warships. More than 300 years earlier the Mary Rose sank as she turned in the channel of water near to the spitbank sands.

APPENDIX 3 – GLOSSARY OF TERMS

Abeam	At right angles to the ship.
Blocks	Wooden pulley blocks.
Bowsprit	Mast extending forwards from the bow.
Carrack	Three or four-masted vessel with high superstructures fore and aft.
Carvel	Hull construction method with planks butting together.
Clinker-built	Hull construction method with planking overlapping.
Foc'sle	The raised forecastle near the bow.
Foremast	First mast from the front.
Galleon	Medium-sized warship propelled by sail.
Galley	Oar-powered ship, or a ship's kitchen.
Gun	The ship's cannon.
Hold	Storage area located in the lowest level of the hull.
Larboard	Old term for the port side of the ship, to the left when looking forward.
Magazine	Storage area for explosives.
Mainmast	Central, tallest mast.

Mizzenmast	Mast behind the mainmast, the third from the front.
Orlop	Storage and living area below the waterline.
Round shot	Cast-iron 'cannonballs'.
Running rigging	Used to hoist and adjust the sails.
Standing rigging	Rigging that supports the masts and bowsprit.
Starboard	Right-hand side of the ship when looking forward.
Tops	A platform where the top mast is attached to the lower mast.
Yards	Horizontal cross pieces from which the square sails are hung.

Other titles available in this series

ISBN 978 07524 5605 8

ISBN 978 07524 5094 0

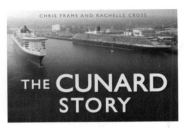

ISBN 978 07524 5914 1

ISBN 978 07524 5092 6

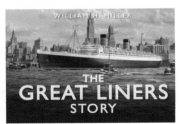

ISBN 978 07524 6452 7

ISBN 978 07524 6404 6